A Hat to Stop a Train

A Hat to Stop a Train

Sheila Stewart

Sheila Stewart

Wolsak and Wynn . Toronto

April 2007

Dear Suzanne,
I look forward to
your book and hope
you enjoy this one.
all the best,
Sheila
Toronto
(One Earth Community
Sharing Our Stories)

Typeset in Garamond, printed in Canada by The Coach House Printing Company, Toronto.

Cover design: Coach House
Author's photograph by Liz Szynkowski

Some of these poems have appeared in *The Antigonish Review, Canadian Woman Studies, Contemporary Verse 2, Descant, Fireweed, Grain, Kaleidoscope, lichen, The Malahat Review, Pottersfield Portfolio, Room of One's Own, Surface & Symbol, Tessera, Windsor Review,* and *WRIT* and in the anthology *A Room at the Heart of Things,* Elisabeth Harvor, ed.

The publishers and the author
gratefully acknowledge the support
of the Canada Council for the Arts
and the Ontario Arts Council.

The Canada Council | Le Conseil des Arts   ONTARIO ARTS COUNCIL
for the Arts | du Canada   CONSEIL DES ARTS DE L'ONTARIO

The author thanks the City of Toronto for its support through a grant from the Toronto Arts Council.

Wolsak and Wynn Publishers Ltd.
192 Spadina Avenue, Suite 315
Toronto, ON
Canada M5T 2C2

National Library of Canada Cataloguing in Publication Data

Stewart, Sheila, 1959-
    A hat to stop a train / Sheila Stewart.

Poems.
ISBN 0-919897-89-4

    I. Title.

PS8587.T4896H38 2003   C811'.6   C2003-901954-3
PR9199.4.S745H38 2003

For Rachel and Maya Stewart Pathak

In memory of Winifred Louise Stewart (1919-1994)

Contents

Callings

Glossary

Acknowledgements

TROUBLES

LADYBONES

Why do I think of your collarbone, what can I make of it? A flute, a
whistle, smooth like your bone-handled knives, the good set tucked away in
a felt bag, the everyday ones growing yellow. I want to know its exact
shape, want to rub it smooth, bone gone to ashes, ashes far away, nothing
in my hand. The bones the Swazi healers threw to tell us our future, what
to do, whom to appease, the bones of ancestors rising up to cast our lot, a
bone falling from a tree.

I think of you dry as a bone. Are you thirsty, do I pick out the bones of the
story?

And your son's bones? Bones with osteomyelitis, bones falling, bones that
broke, that left him with a brace on his leg, so you said, *keep it out of sight for
the photo.*

Why do I want you, *Skinamalink Malone, Skinny Bones?* You, the slim,
delicate one, your father said, *every farm should be able to support one lady,* your
lady bones. My wishbone.

Hipbones letting forth daughters, my bones open and loose, how I shake
them, spine elongated, a hundred bony bones in this hand moving.

EDGEWISE

What happens when you're the narrator, but you can't help shrinking and slipping off the page, words and story so slippery, wanting to escape the same-old, same-old?

It's hard to get a word in edgewise when the big ones are all gabbing like a barnyard family, one goose, two chickens, three goats, a dog and a cat. So many and you need them to reach you down a glass of water.

You're back a bouncy baby on a lap. Aiming those piercing eyes wherever you like. No one has told you yet that it's rude to stare and what the eye can see. Everyone is so happy to have a baby, such a distraction, you suck it all up. They don't know you can taste the aspirin ground up in the spoonful of strawberry jam. So small you fit in the pauses between words, you see between the blinds and right up under the curtains, you can spy from any cupboard. But no need really: you know what the visitors do when Mummy leaves the room.

You can hold onto the last word of a sentence only so long. They say, *you'll be a big girl soon*, but your fat baby legs help you slide along the edge of the next paragraph.

Perfect baby ears hear the space around grandfather's clock, the old grey goose, the sound of the iron heating, the moment before the camera's click.

SIGNS OF HER

The stockings she put in the drawer, two grey hairs
on the high ruffled collar of a navy blouse, a Kleenex
in the pocket of a plaid skirt, small white and pink
mints in a black clutch purse.

I am sorting her outfits into four piles: keep, give
to a friend, send to Ireland, Salvation Army. Trying
on her Donegal tweed suit, wrapped in what's left.

I want to try on the way she calmly banged
the brass gong as husband's and son's voices exploded
around the room, stopping them short, the way
she said, *they have no power over me*, the way she wrapped
my nightie around a hot water bottle, left it on my pillow with
a note, the way she packed my lunch of wheaten salad sandwiches,
crusts cut off, the way she said about a trifle with raspberries,
strawberries, custard and cream, *it goes round my heart like velvet.*

Finely crocheted white lace collars in the drawer.
I could fill the pockets with notes.
What I know:
bought at Norma Bradley's Dress Shop in Waterloo, wore
to Ireland in the winter of 1991, held her first grandchild
on her lap in this pleated skirt, this sleeveless dress worn on
a warm summer evening in 1975 when she spread out a table-cloth,
opened a wicker picnic basket by the lake at Goderich.

Two round hat boxes, her clothes on the empty bed, my
photo in her wallet, my photo beside a pile of hankies folded
in triangles in the top drawer, my name on a small name tag
in her jewelry box, one left over after she had sewn
the others onto the inside of my collars.

What I know and don't know about her.

HER BODY STILL

I don't want this to be part
of your memory, the nurse said, pulling
the curtain around my mother's cooling
body, your memory mine
        hers, her body hers

mine. Her memories flown
        out the blank hospital window over
Lake Ontario, thin and cool
        like the paper under her half-glass of water,
flown away to lodge in the whin bushes
        covering the Mountains of Mourne, all
she didn't tell held between the fingers
        of her hot-cold hands. Memory lying still
                        in her dry mouth.

THE LADIES AND THE BOMB

The Royal Doulton figurines standing on the mantlepiece aren't touched by the bomb exploding outside. The policeman and his family who live across the street are away in Spain. On Costa del Sol television they see that their house is destroyed. Not an ash falls on the white skin, coiffured hair, or ruffled dresses of the ladies. The one in the yellow dress tilts her head to the left, her hand brushes her cheek. The one in the green pinafore and matching hat lifts her skirt to reveal her many petticoats. She raises her eyes, the front window shatters.

ULSTER WEDDING

We were told of your wedding
in a line at the end of Aunt Mary's letter.

At ten, you and I
played on your farm overlooking
the Maze Prison.

At night the lights of Long Kesh lit the sky,
the guard dogs barked.

We weren't invited to your wedding.
Among the relatives
you are never mentioned.
Though no one ever said
we know you married a Catholic.

DRESSING

If only I'd known
it was going to be such an ugly box I'd have
brought an Irish linen tablecloth to
place over it.
                          Ugly as hell, my father said, but he
is a practical man.

                                        Nobody saw that box
except my dad, the funeral attendants, my brother and me.
Dad wasn't going to be taken advantage of
by a funeral home
                          but my mother loved beautiful things.

                          We spoke to Mum of Glen Farm
her sisters, Hillsborough, Ahoghill
kissed that box
each of us
my father first
after he read from the Bible.
He'd spent his life conducting church services.

                    I sat beside Mum in the pew.
She would take two mints from her purse
one for me and one for her.
                          We would suck them.
At the end of the last hymn
it was my job to check her breath
she would breathe on my upturned face: *haa*

VISITATION I

Mother summons me to church so we can be together. She waits for us in the pew, helps me settle myself and the girls.

She whispers, *It never did a person any harm to get out to church. It may be you come to see me, but I'm sure you and the girls are getting something out of it. Even if you don't dress properly, you're looking very well.* I pull at my black cords, glance at wrinkles down the front of my green turtleneck. I gaze at her style, the angle of her spring hat, matching purse and gloves. I can't even keep up with the seasons. The congregation pales beside her.

When it's time to pass the Peace of Christ and shake the hands of our fellow parishioners, she's off to seek out the lonely and elderly. She herself has grown young and spry. Then she's back, sitting beside me, waiting so still for me to open the hymnal and lean towards her, our fingers cradling the spine.

AFTER

I
After the funeral there's the tidying up
sorting out throwing out
    who gets what   who should get what
why   who loved her   best
least   was loved best   least   helped
    her most   least   was hurt
most   deserves the most   least   needs
    the most   was given

                                    least.

Who gets to do the tidying up
gets left with it
gets the good dishes
the blue vase.

II
After the tidying up – as if
we go to a tidy place called After –
who gets to talk to Dad
who's around who's available who's
far away who calls who
doesn't.

Who visits Father who
remembers their anniversary
who remembers what who
gives a damn.

III
After supper we watched closely as she
cut the pumpkin pie
dished out the slices
evenly. After kindergarten came lunch,
after lunch was afternoon, after noon
she was mine.

ENTERTAINING

In the trunk of the car
which she'd call the boot
is the urn, her ashes
and a pile of her portraits.
She is twenty-one
splendid in a long dark gown
there beside the brush that cleans
the snow off the window.

Home from the memorial service
we entertain her friends –
some lively, others vague and withdrawn.
Her best plates set out
on her favourite white and green linen,
tea served in her Limoges cups.
Phyllis says, *you're the image of your mother.*

After they go we lift
the lid of the trunk.

THE BELFAST TELEGRAPH

We were far from Belfast in Tandragee, my father's birthplace, not in
Hillsborough, my mother's village. A married daughter isn't buried with
her parents. Hillsborough is where Mum watched the Queen, saw her over
the wall of the castle, Mum and the Queen, girls at the same time. Mum
named her second son Charles after the prince born on the same day.

Tandragee is far from Belfast with its battle dates on the walls. The dates on
the tombstones tell us of people who died of old age, illness, car accidents.
Only one policeman killed in the Troubles in Tandragee, which is far from
Belfast.

We were far from Belfast where fighting breaks out at funerals, the
opposing side taunts the mourners, the police check to see who attends
which funerals. No one checked us in Tandragee. One son attended, the
other didn't. People who were barely talking passed each other with furled
umbrellas tucked tight underarm. No cease-fire there either.

It was raining slightly so the Glen Farm boys – four middle-aged men –
were able to come. It wasn't a day for haying. I was glad about the rain
though I don't know what to say to men with farmers' hands.

My favourite cousin said she would look out for Mum. She'd take the road
past the plain Presbyterian church on the way from work. *These young ones
commute all the way to Belfast you know.* She'd look out for Mum, she said, stop
in with her where she rests in Tandragee.

We were flying further away from Tandragee, when I read my mother's
obituary in *The Belfast Telegraph*, "The National Newspaper of Northern
Ireland" though few Catholics buy it. *Shortsighted? A Simple Outpatient
Treatment Carried Out World-wide.* An LVF car bomb explosion outside the
Sinn Fein office. Royal Irish Regiment Recruiting Drive. Price-Beater
Deals for Cregagh Carpets. Peace Talks in Trouble. Weather Warming.

NO WASH

Great-aunt Elsie lay in bed for years in her coat and Wellington boots, laughing during the night. She left her bed only to shout from the window, at her brothers James and John, long dead. On our holiday at Aunt Mary's, Mum and I slept in the room along the hall from Great-aunt Elsie. I held my breath and took in her morning cup of tea, *Home Sweet Home* in needlepoint on her wall. *Mary? No, you must be Winifred home from Canada.* I didn't correct her, her mouth a dark hole. Came out, gasping for breath.

If Aunt Elsie had raised her eyes from James and John in the yard and looked over the field, she might have seen Long Kesh, barbed wire linking the four towers. The prisoners clothed only in their blankets drew the spiral of New Grange and the Gaelic convolutions of the Book of Kells in their faeces on the walls. Crucifixes at their necks. Something to die for. Messages to prisoners in the local paper: *Blessed are they who hunger and thirst for justice.*

The prisoners' *No Wash Protest*, but to us, the Scots-Irish, more British than the Brits, the *Dirty Protest*. Aunt Mary wouldn't call it anything at all, wouldn't mention it. How would she think of it, when after her morning devotions, the radio listed their names?

I watched the milking, the border collie Susie, blind in one eye, herding the cows in. I brought a jug of warm milk to Aunt Mary, then helped her stir the batter for a table of fruit-loaves at the Moravian Garden Party. Money to be raised for the next famine in Africa.

Mary had much to do: take Elsie her breakfast, tell her about the calving, try to persuade her to bathe. *Come down for your tea today, for the Canadian relatives, just say hello to the young ones.*

Great-aunt Elsie could have stepped high over the threshold of her bedroom doorway as if avoiding broken glass, gone downstairs, out the kitchen door, if she'd had a mind to. One of her lanky grandsons would have stopped her before she got too far. At haying time, she used to head Long Kesh way to take her men their tea. These days she filled her hands with bed-sheets, working those bed-sheets as if kneading bread dough.

Across the fields, behind the towers, a mother held a young man's hand, a sheet shrouding his shrunken frame. She whispered, "Wouldn't you drink a little, Son?"

He could barely make out her face as he whispered, "Go. Go!"

KNITTED

Can you find me? my father asks, passing me his old school photograph – the schoolyard in Tandragee – his stranger's face, rough and tough, among rows of boys, looks like he'd been in a brawl that day – you better watch out. *I hated that pullover. Look at the sleeves, they change colour half-way down. My mother ran out of wool, finished a fine blue pullover in brown.* I study the faces to find his brothers, my father's finger traces the dead.

I've settled down in an armchair at the library, every book on Ireland piled beside me. What am I looking for in this book on the Troubles? One photograph detains me: a crowd of boys lined up, bigger ones at the back, jacket hoods up, scarves over their faces, dark glasses on a few. *Members of the Ulster Defence Association.* In the second row, a knitted pullover, a hanky tied bandit-style. My finger touches his image, I want to see his face.

NOT A BODY ABOUT

She bought herself good clothes out of the housekeeping
money, paying on instalment, trying them on for
me. She'd produce them from the back

of the closet, say to Dad, *you mean you haven't seen
this old thing.* I'd help her choose earrings, a necklace.
I stand in her room, a museum. My well-turned-out

mother, the flat surface of a photograph. I had my
daughters in time to take her picture with them, put her
where I can see her in a frame she'd like. I dress the

baby and my big girl says, *I want to dress you.* My mother's
mother used to say, *not a body about to help me dress.* Do up
the zipper.

DRESS

You left me a thin flowered dress and a box of hankies. I can sit in your dress, sleeveless in the Canadian winter. Put it on and head to a strawberry social. Thank my lucky stars I'm in a pretty dress just my size. They can look and say, hey, she's been to a lady's dress shop in downtown Ontario.

I could sniff around the entrances of dress shops, or glide in the way you did. Never bat an eyelid at the prices. Pretend royalty.

Or I can sit in your dress and play with my box of hankies. A blue Birks' box about the size of a bread and butter plate. Take them out one by one, examine the embroidered garden scenes, the tatted edges, fold them up again, put them back. I could iron them all. Fold them in triangles. Sort them in piles. And crumple them. Use them as face cloths, dish cloths. Dirty them. Throw them out the windows of trains. Toss them like confetti from the top of the Royal York Hotel.

I'd still have the dress: I could hoist it up a flagpole. Hello, air. Let it grow grey, limp. Or yank it down. Pull out the threads one by one, bare the interfacing, rip out the zipper, knock its teeth crooked. Cut on the bias, it might rip real nice and smooth down the middle, or around the waist.

Rip it up, or cut it. You'd prefer I use pinking shears to cut zigzag edges in perfect circles, like the gingham ones that top jam jars at the Kitchener market.

Any scissors would do. Scraps of dress. Reds, greens, pinks. Purple poppies, variegated leaves, snips of stem.

A perfect plate for a tiny scone beaded with the red of strawberries.

LETTERS

READING THE BLUES

She called them Blues. *Any*
Blues? Thin blue
airmail letters from her sisters.
Any Blues? she'd call
to whoever brought in the mail. Sometimes
we'd pretend there were none, then draw them
from pockets or sleeves with
a flourish, or present them on a silver
tray – *voila!* – with a cup of tea and a digestive
biscuit. *Any Blues?* she'd call from her bed.

What do we do with Blues?
Smell them, hold them tight,
read them slow, tuck them
under a pillow to re-read at night.

She wasn't a lady to cry
the blues. What didn't she say
to me, or herself? What can you tell
a mother anyway? Unwritten letters. *Don't go*
crying, she'd say.

What we tell
each other: a pale
picture, a slight blue.

IN MILK

I

We played at weddings down the Glen Road, had to get the lace curtains out the door without Granny seeing. I remember the nine of us in procession one day – how we all got out of the chores I don't know. We held the reception in the barn with the pigs. That was long before we were in milk. We went into milk in the 1930s. My brother James delivered milk all the way to Belfast, stopped in at the Armagh Bakery, was given cream buns for us wee ones.

II

Granny used to love to see us all dressed up. Couldn't let Daddy know though, he didn't approve of dances. Granny would say, "Child dear, have you not a bit of a bodice? Your back is all bare. I'll lend you a bodice, don't you know." Mummy wouldn't have let on to Daddy. She'd let us go to things. Past midnight, she'd run her hands over the beds to see that we were all there.

A HAT TO STOP A TRAIN

My mother was a woman who could wear a hat.
She stepped out the door in a deep pink number
pink netting gathered over flowers and bows
matching up-to-the-elbow gloves.

Tam, pillbox, bird's nest, broad-brimmed
wedding hats, funeral hats
hats for outings to the seaside.

A hat to emigrate in.

I have her octagonal hatboxes
chequered cream and beige, flowered
dusty boxes with tissue-wrapped hats.

First to decay is the powder blue.
It moults blue feathers like the budgie.
Tiny labels intact inside the bands:
By Sanje
Splendid Sealskin
United Hatters, Millinery Workers
Union Made in USA.

A lady can go far in the right hat
in just the hat for the occasion:
turquoise and lime with a bow off to the left.
A hat to stop a train.

TIGHT

Was it my mother's fault that she bound me to her tight? Her sisters lived
far away, her cousins too, her childhood friends. Who does a minister's
wife talk to anyway? Needy parishioners on the phone. One spoke so loud
that we could hear her voice across the room. Mum held the phone six
inches away from her ear, nodded at her and me.

When I was clearing out the house, I found my old letters home from
Swaziland. They were not about Swaziland. They were about *I hope you are
okay, don't get sick while I am far away, whatever you do keep living until I get home
and we are having a lovely time here with the Irish midwives and I've told them all about
you and they take great care of us and we have them over for lovely meals and I made
scones and wheaten bread and brownies showed the nurses how to make lasagna they
make a fruit-loaf very like yours and they have us over they are such good craic and there
are lots of parties and visits these Irish nurses are my sisters taking care of me and I hope
Dad is taking care of you and I'll be home soon and don't worry a thing about me I'm
sorry to be so far away but we are having a lovely time so lovely wish you were here and
I'll write again soon.*

TIGHTER

Who else was there to wind those elastic bandages around her legs? She only had one daughter, one son was far away, and what do you ask a son to do anyway? A woman copes as well as she can on her own. Doesn't complain. Certainly doesn't tell everyone everything. Not the details. Even to her doctor, won't burden him – nice tidy young man who's very busy – wouldn't show him her legs unless she had to.

When I wound those elastic bandages around your legs, you said, *not too tight, a little tighter.* You said to me, *you'd make such a lovely nurse, such a kind bedside manner.* I was so good at rubbing in cream, paring corns. You preferred me to use a blade, not a file, and I did my best not to draw blood. After your legs were all bandaged up, I helped you pull on your toeless elastic stockings. Later you had the ones with zippers up the back.

You didn't complain and you didn't like to ask; you'd say, *I wish there were someone to go and get me my slippers. Who else was there to wind those elastic bandages around your legs?*

LIONS AND CASTLES

I'm a *Mlungo*, a white, in the Swazi part of the Bend Inn. A man from Maputo leans on the bar and tells me the long story of his decline, the only time in my life I understand Portuguese perfectly, a bottle of Lion in my hand, a tin of Castle in his. Miriam Makeba on the jukebox, *Pata Pata*. Lucky Dube. *Skorokoro*. *Red Red Wine*.

The week before, I drove my small red truck into the Lubombo Mountain Range, to see the lights of Maputo across the border. Manuel, my best student, had slipped across. We said goodbye not knowing if he would make it there or back.

I dance round and loose here, dance all night: lions and castles. On the white side of the bar, they sit. On the other side of the world, my mother sits reading my letter, which tells nothing.

TWO CHAIRS

I'm edging closer to her, putting
down words because when I showed her a poem
I'd written about her, she smiled,
ach, it's about me.

      Trouble is there wasn't enough about her,
      only her wedding and her funeral.

I'm pulling up two chairs
laying down words, side by side
                    my side by her side.
She's telling me about Glen Farm
the two Miss Hutchinsons coming for tea.
They were seated with their backs to the fire
a row of wee Ward girls, Mum and her sisters,
when opposite them Annie Hutchinson slurped her tea.
The girls with a case of the giggles
their chairs too close
couldn't get out, Mum in the middle.
I'm trying to edge
closer. If only I could be one
of the Ward girls getting ready for a party
making scones, pavlovas, Victorian sandwiches
Mary the sweet,
Evelyn the savoury.
When they brought home Catholic boys
they changed the surnames.

Mum's boyfriend Leonard, a soldier from Wales,
sang to her, but her parents said he was from too far away
so she wrote to him calling it off.

The very next day, at home, in a new royal blue dress, she met
the young minister who would take her away to Canada. Her friend
Maureen McKinney arrived with a carload of ministers knowing Mum
was partial to men in suits or uniforms. Dad took her first
to the Presbyterian manse at Ahoghill, County Antrim.
A huge empty manse they had to furnish on 300 a year.

Antrim accents ring of Scotland from the time of the *confiscation*
or *plantation*, a Catholic word and a Protestant word.

What did she say when he first talked about leaving Ireland?
She didn't want to go. Her father cried as he stood at the doorway
when they passed that morning on the way to the boat.

> Trouble is she missed
> the weddings and funerals.

Putting down words like planting bulbs one after the other or cutting out
scones on a floured board, placing them down on the baking sheet close to
each other, thickest ones at the edges so they won't burn, I'm putting down
words trying to get closer to her, to sit with her or lie down beside her on
the bed piled high with pillows, putting down words because her ashes are
away in Ireland. I don't have a place to visit her.

THINGS SHE TAUGHT ME

My mother taught me how to make butter
curls and melon balls, how to put on nylon
stockings, rub hand-cream into my hands
like pulling on a pair of gloves.

How to write an essay:
just put on your best bib and tucker, dear
and type it up.

The last thing she said to my father
it was still dark:
pull the blankets over me.

Pull the blankets over me, dear
I add the "dear."
Mother showed me
how when you lift
the baby out of the crib at night
draw the bed-sheets up again
to keep that spot warm.

I'VE JUST MADE YOUR LUNCH

I've just made your lunch, Dad
set our places across
the kitchen table from each other
put out mushroom soup and
a cheese and tomato sandwich.
Stronger tea than Mum made.

On the phone, you say
I have to get my own lunch
wash the dishes
I can't get used to being alone.

When we sit down to eat, you say,
we haven't done this for years
just the two of us together
but we do it each month
when I come to town because
I don't bring the children much.

Your grandchildren eat too slow
they dribble their soup.

VISITATION II

How did she manage to find me in a community centre washroom right before the literacy committee meeting? She tapped me on the shoulder as I washed my hands and glanced at myself in the mirror.

You look good in my green scarf, she said. *Claire sent me that one. She always remembered my birthday. Now about your clothes, Dear, please keep ringing the changes. You always did have your favourites and I could hardly get you out of them.*

How kind of her to track me down on a day when I'd missed the streetcar and burdened myself with too many files. I want coffee after reading three years' worth of minutes on the King streetcar. *Try to get a little extra rest, Sweetie, and don't worry about a thing. You look so lovely, it doesn't matter what you say.* She could be my sister with the same wide smile, even better than my imaginary friend who I always beat in races along the hall.

If it doesn't matter what I say, Sis, what if I say nothing at all? It's taken me a lifetime to start talking and I still don't like it – speech is such a muddy compromise. At a crowded meeting, let me be the fly on the wall, the ghost in the bathroom set free.

TEA TOWEL NO. 5

A young girl steps toward the sea, barefoot,
a letter in her hand. Behind her the Mountains

of Mourne rise from the shore. She looks out
over the bay – her hair, cape and skirt shifting in the breeze.

A fisherman in a small boat. All is pictured on
a green tea towel. Above the church spire,

a map of County Down floats in the sky, red dots dropped
along the shore for Moira, Ballywalter, Chapeltown, Grossdrumman,

Ringboy, Annalong. Clustered inland Hillsborough, Dromore, Drumbeg,
and Dromara. *Tea towel no. 5 in the series.*

Would she sing the words in the letter, know the tune in the linen sky?
Oh Mary! This London's a wonderful sight!

ON THE TRAIN

from Belfast to Dublin we pass the
village where he was born. He doesn't notice. He's

telling the history of Ireland in a clear loud voice, too
loud for the train from Belfast to Dublin. As Armagh

and Drogheda pass through the window he speaks
of men made martyrs. We forget to look for

the village on the hill, castle turned potato
crisp factory, the store they lived above, linen mill,

tenement houses, the pump, the boy drawing water,
delivering papers. Midwife Miss Mason, a big

woman riding her bicycle up the hill, stops to ask
the child his name and says, *you are one of mine.*

THE RIGHT PATH

Listen, we sold our furniture and carpets in an auction.
I made the decision for all of us. Everyone thought
we were crazy emigrating at our age. You never know
which path is right. Life isn't meant to be simple.

I made the decision for all of us. Everyone thought
how hard on my wife to leave her family.
Life isn't meant to be easy. Which path is right?
Our homeland's brewing war.

How hard on your mother to leave her family.
Could I have made a difference?
Our homeland's brewing war.
A hair's breadth, a prayer for peace.

Could I have made a difference?
Were we crazy emigrating at our age? You never
know. A hair's breadth, a prayer for peace. I watched
as the auctioneer sold our furniture and carpets.

IT WASN'T ME

who left
*the Ballymena Manse, packed up my two small sons, arm in my
husband's, stepped onto the boat. Landed in Montreal, took a train
to Toronto, followed my sons from one car to the next, as they rubbed
their good clothes along the floor.* Not me *arriving in Brechin, walking
through the rooms of our new house, thank goodness the church ladies had
made up the beds. Dinner at a parishioner's home and we watched to
see how Canadians eat corn still on the cob.* Not me

*back at Carnlough, sitting mid a row of my friends, arms folded in our laps,
husbands standing behind. There between Lily and Evelyn, ocean salt spraying
our hair.* That's not *my first-born in the arms of his cousin.* Not me *with my
mother. Here with an arm around each niece. Luminous at the Ordination Day
of my husband-to-be.* Not me *picnicking at Curlingford Castle, in front of the
Round Tower at Navan. Me sitting in the long grass with Josephine at
Portstewart, eyes on the ocean. At Bradda Glen, in front of Balmoral Hotel,
the Isle of Man, Ballyferris.* I wasn't there. *The Sunday School picnic, my
wide-brimmed hat, our big circle at Blackrock Beach.*

PRAYERS

GONE TO GHOST

She's a face looking
at the Giant's Causeway in a book
called *Ireland.* She's a young girl standing

on a five-sided rock looking
at giants. She's a hand over my mouth. She's
a figment who doesn't lie. She's a cloth doll waiting

to be told. She's a woman who steps into an antique
store and asks to see fire irons. She's a lady
examining the fire-arms they brought

her, declaring them unsuitable. She's the hero
of this story, a lady who looks rifles, handguns
and antique dealers in the eye. She's an empty

napkin ring with my name on it. She's a hand over
my hand, a giant gone to ghost, a stream
of words pushing the air around me.

AT THE DROP OF A HAT

Would you come to the table, please? Dad and I carry in the bowls. *Would you like more soup? Have you had enough?*

She opens the doors and ushers
in the multitude.

As she unpins her hat, she plans the menu. Gathers up orphans, the lonely, bereaved. Rustles up lunch for fifteen as she arrives home from church. Warms their bones.

Mrs. Patterson says, *this soup cures more than a cold,* as her hand shakes the spoon towards her mouth.

She feeds a crowd at the drop of a hat. She lifts labelled casseroles from the full freezer. *Dear, would you please set out the teacups?* Orange jellied salad wobbles onto a bed of iceberg lettuce. I cut carrot and celery sticks, put out pickles – it's better in here than with the crowd of adults filling the living room with questions. I drop a garnish of parsley on the pink rolled-up slices of ham, Dad preaches in the living room.

Right after lunch I'll get away.

She lifts the loaves, looks out into
the backyard, drops of rain on the clothesline.
Come and be seated, she commands.
She breaks bread.
Everyone eats and is filled.

WHAT CAN YOU TELL?

I

Not this: the boys grabbed me as I got off the bus from school just at the end of Glen Road so close to home why Lily wasn't with me that day I don't know   where could she have gone?

I didn't know those boys don't know if they were from the Catholic school don't remember uniforms

there were three of them one about my age and two bigger I was in my uniform just handed down to me from Lily   it was still good

I thought they were going to kill me   do God knows what   but they were in a hurry pushed me into the *schoch* nettles stinging my legs and arms down on my hands and knees dirt stuffed up my nose and into my mouth off they ran laughing   I didn't make a sound   straw   dirt   stones in my mouth   too scared   snot running

can't remember   how I made it up Glen Road   blouse and stockings ripped   thorns in my legs   throat raw   Mary saw me from the barn got me all washed   said   we won't   tell   the others   won't worry them not even Mummy   *the less said the better*

II

I wasn't right since   one thing leads to another   a couple weeks later I was in bed with rheumatic fever   didn't get back to school for a year   my sisters and brothers came upstairs sat by my bed one after the other rheumatic fever led to my heart troubles   sure I put a brave face on   put it out of my mind   these things come to try you   *one thing leads to another*

III

        a story she didn't tell   (the less said)   a stone
             sitting silent   didn't tell a daughter   told a son
                           her frail self
                                    letting loose

   words
        falling
            from
               her

all she didn't tell me
    all I didn't tell her   our mouths full
                          stones

ETTA HOLDING MY HAND

one of them might have been the size of the young MacFadden boy they
were always rough   I thought I saw him one day at Port Rush staring at me
I was with my big sisters Etta and Mary

my big sisters could do the work of men
milking calving haying

us wee ones   Lily   Lucy   and I were up in
Etta's room making tea for our dolls   the fire lit in the hearth   Mummy
was furious at us disturbing Etta in her sickbed   I was big for dolls   just
messing with the others

I was the delicate one, but Etta was the one to
die   not yet twenty-one   consumption   they always said Daddy never got
over it

that boy staring
I didn't look back

holding my hand

CARDINALS

The boys and Dad in browns and greys, his clerical
collar white at his throat. Though colour

has arrived in this 1960s photo: Mum and I matching
in our red dresses, her black heels still, my round-toed
  shoes dangling toward the carpet. Two cardinals accidentally
  among the sparrows.

I look and look
at the tiny point where my
   hand could be holding hers. Hers are clasped on her lap.
   I'm sitting on mine, but I look again, and

   she searches for my eight-year-old hand, her warm
fingers take mine,
lost in red plumage,
   her vast wings closed about her. Wait,

wings beating at the window, we perch on the windowsill
  a moment. Look, and away.

SERVICE

Mum touches my knee to make me stop swinging my feet beneath the pew. Her shiny, black purse sits between us. Mum touches my hand when I fidget and shuffle. She looks at me when I bang the pew in front by mistake.

She used to bring me a little notebook to draw and write in. Now I read the bulletin, the little offering envelopes, the welcome card for visitors, *Alpha and Omega* above the organ pipes. I use the red ribbon attached to the hymnbook to mark the first hymn and envelopes for the others. I count the men and women in the choir, the bald heads, the glasses. When the choir stands to sing, I watch the orange smudge of lipstick on Mrs. Thrasher's front teeth.

Then we get to stand up and sing. Taking a deep breath, I belt out the hymn. Mum's tone deaf. When she went to piano lessons, her teacher taught her how to cover butter boxes instead. Mum mouths the words. Sometimes, I hear a small thin voice coming from her. Mum likes to hear me sing. She says it drowns out her mistakes.

RITUALS

Our father is getting ready for a funeral. On Saturdays it's weddings. He always leaves it a bit late. The house is panicked; we stay out of his way, making sure not to hold up the bathroom. Mother lays out his clothes, black shirt and white collar, ironed handkerchief, socks to match his dark suit. He has misplaced his watch and prayer book; I'm sent to fetch them.

The black car pulls up and I answer the doorbell embarrassed that our father isn't ready. Young slick funeral attendants are always in twos and don't come in, thank God. They stand beside the long black car, its engine still running. I peer at them from behind the curtain and wonder about the dead. Who found the body? Were the eyes open? I don't suppose those men dress the body. I guess a family member would do that. Father says that funeral directors are a money-making crew preying upon people at their most vulnerable time.

Our father rushes to the door. A moment ago he was rushing along the hall in his underwear. He steps outside with a certain presence, long black coat and fresh white scarf, prayer book in hand.

THE MANSE COMMITTEE

Be tidy and clean and quiet and good. The manse committee is on its way.
Ordinary, kind-enough folk with a higher destiny to inspect the house,
assess the wear of carpets and the age of appliances, see what's to be done.
They can't help but notice the shiny windowsills and polished door handles.
If the manse committee, heaven forbid, saw dirt, heard noise, found a
problem, noticed the worst, they would know that we are really a sinful, lazy
lot of unbelievers who put elbows on the table, talk with our mouths full,
lick butter knives, gossip about the congregation members, pass wind in the
living room. Perhaps they'd suspect that the minister smokes cigarettes in
the bathroom, the son steals condoms from the top drawer of the minister's
chest-of-drawers, and the daughter plays doctor with the kids next door.

THE MINISTER'S WIFE RETIRES

No more preparing a hot and cold
buffet for the choir. No more Sunday

School picnics. No more inviting the lonely and
bereaved for lunch after church. No more baking

up a storm for Church Teas. No more luncheons for
Communion Class, teas for Sunday School teachers. No

more starching white collars. No
more making sure there is Welch's grape juice

in the cupboard for communion to be taken to
the shut-ins. No more quiet listening and careful

nodding to the minister when he gets home from
the Official Board meetings. No more, she crowed,

reclining in the Lazyboy. *I've retired too.*

VISITATION III

My study is my space, though also the guest-room, and the space that my seven-year-old wants as her very own room, doesn't want to share with her sister anymore. One morning, I walk in and who should be waking up there but Mum. Her face framed by two or three pillows. Her hairnet on.

"Hello, Darling," she says, sits up in bed and begins taking out her curlers, setting curlers and bobby-pins on my tall pile of books. *Irish Tales for the Telling.* She'd like that. *Feminist Parenting.* Hem. *Erotic Interludes.* At least it's far down the pile.

I ease into the desk chair not wanting to disturb a thing, take a long look at my beautifully wrinkled, not-yet-frail mother. Wouldn't you know it – *A Hat to Stop a Train* is out on the desk, and Mum often reads a bit, at about three in the morning, if she can't sleep. Offending lines spring to mind. Why on earth had I written about her legs? Should I take out everything about Dad, or perhaps I didn't mention him enough?

I can't find any words, but she replies as if I'd asked, "No, I slept perfectly. Lovely to see this *women of the Bible* quilt again. The church ladies made it and presented it to me for our twenty-fifth wedding anniversary."

There are even poems I'd left out, right there in rows across the bed. Her legs resting under them had shifted them ever so slightly, but Mum had been sleeping under quilted panels and borders of fish and crosses, Mary, Martha, Miriam, the Queen of Sheba. I ease myself over pages, around her, and crawl in beside her, stroke her arm, soft and slack. Smooth downy hairs.

She smells the same, Jo-curl, wheaten bread, heaven.

HURRY UP

Her wrist, thin
in my fist, she doesn't
do what I say,
doesn't eat her cheese on toast,
drink her apple juice,
put her shoes on.
Get your shoes on, we'll be late
hurry up, now.
She's talking
humming.
I'm trying to keep
a fist
from my words
trying not to
squeeze her thinness,
shake   her.

She's sitting
at the bottom of the stairs
looking for the hole
in the leg of her tights.
A small white moon on a navy thigh.

FLOWERED DRESS OR FLOWER GARDEN?

Easier to look at the dress than the garden. So close at hand. A dress with history. (And I didn't cut it to pieces.) Already ironed. Round neck, straight lines. All done, not like the garden. Forsythia and dogwood needing a trim. Too many daylilies. Laburnum, lobelia. Mint gone mad. Ferns so you can't find the path. But this indoor poet needs out.

A dress hanging on the back of a door. Its flowers don't move except with breeze through the window.

A dress waiting to dance. Stroll to the lake. Dress will float its flowers, flip them round the Royal Canadian Legion dance floor, the vintage D-day posters unflappable, lean on the patio railing, sailboats moored at the dock. A Lake Ontario breeze through the window. Hand on its back. Petals fly.

THE FRONT ROW

Let me be eight. Let me slip in between Mum and Lily over
        to the left in the front row, join the family portrait on the

mantle. Five wee Ward girls up front. I'd be the sixth.
        Mary and Etta would get me ready for the photo, it's still

the year before Etta died. They'd have a dress ready for me
        in the closet, black leather shoes, thick cream

stockings. Let me disappear in Ireland, into the Troubles,
        into my aunt's parlour, into all that *craic*

with a gathering of the cousins. *Sure, there's no holding back*
        Evelyn when she has her mind made up.

That wee Emily's a going concern. She was up at her Grandma's
        th'day, running after chickens. Let me help Nora

with her catering, hear all the chat while we prepare
        a luncheon in Belfast for five hundred, salmon mousse

the starter. Vicky's brought Alex, just back from Drumcree.
        He was the youngest of four, now of three, one son lost

to a silage machine. Let me go as Claire grips me by the elbow,
        presses a prayer book into my hands. She prays for both

sides, Orangemen and bombers. Can she save me? Play your
        Mum, look your best, they'll never notice

you've gone away and now you are a ghost. After all, they've things
        to say. Listen, you'll hear it all. Let me be

eight. Let me slip.

THEY SAY IT'S GOD WHO HEARS EVERYTHING

I opened Mum's leather-bound *Birthday Book of Friendship* and she began:

> Keep it a secret, but there is a way to meet. On your birthday, the River Mill Restaurant. Sit at the back, the table near the window where we had lunch, just before you went to Africa. Do you remember the lovely salmon? Your back to the door, look out the window: I'll appear when you're ready

I have a birthday present for you – I'm filling a notebook you gave me. You didn't know I could bring anything with me, did you? Recipes at the back – all the ones I had in my head – memories up front. It's time I wrote a little myself. Ask me whatever you want and I might write about it.

Remember, look out the window. Of course, I don't need to eat, but I love the smell of food and a good linen tablecloth.

Give me your poetry book, then, if you want to, and don't worry about a thing. Remember how I used to smooth your brow, kiss your eyes, try to keep the lines from your face.

Don't let on, but I get so much reading done now. I've a special comfortable royal blue chair at the library, and a librarian who brings me just what I want. She's the only one who sees me and she knows what I need.

Keep this right under your hat: *voices*. I hear voices, always have, never told a soul. It doesn't disturb my reading, but when I want to hear, I look out the window. Sweetie, it's not just conversation I hear, it's the whole kit-and-caboodle, much of it not repeatable. Doesn't faze me. Like when your dad was visiting that elderly woman, in the nursing home. She said exactly what was on her mind: *Now here's this stupid minister again. Never liked him. Hope he goes home soon.* People think of everything at the library and I can hear it all. I can tune it in or out, turn it on or off like a radio. I used to pretend to be shocked by bad language, didn't want you to think I was *too* worldly. But, my, the staff in the lunchroom, the public in the washrooms – I hear everything, not just what they say, but what they mean to say, dream of saying, dream of dreaming.

Funny thing, it was the same at church. During the prayers – I prayed too – but I opened my mind to the others' thoughts. Church is peaceful like the library – my, how the mind wanders. They say it's God who hears everything, but sometimes it's the minister's wife. I never told your father, didn't want to alarm him, but it helped me to help him with his work. Gave him a little advice as he went out to his pastoral visits.

I've seen you on the streetcar and at the lounge at the museum, sipping your coffee and pretending to read your book, eavesdropping all the while. Well, you come by it honestly, dear.

We can meet yearly on your birthday. You used to write in those journals and I wondered what you wrote. Now I've time myself. Just you keep it all to yourself. My own version of my life – got to set you straight.

VISITATION IV

We meet secretly, she
   and I. She waits for me
     by the maple, we walk to
      the riverbank, not a soul

in sight. I lay out a plaid
   blanket beneath the willow, open
     a wicker picnic basket, take
      out a flask of tea, bottle of

milk, cubes of sugar, embroidered
   napkins, sprigs of yellow flowers
     in the corners. She sees only
      me. I make her an open-faced

egg-salad sandwich, just how she likes it
   more milky tea, paradise cakes
     filled with raspberry jam. Swans
      come to see us, I let her

feed them a big bag of bread crusts,
   she's my little girl and she's
     not scared, strokes

my hair. *This does me the world
   of good.*

TROUBLES

Ach, you're a wee Ward, your mother
all over again.

Sure I can tell a Catholic
if I pass one   *don't say it*
not just by what street
they're on or by their clothes
– you know – slovenly   *didn't hear it*
it's their eyes too: *don't know it*
so close together.

Sure, they kick with the left
foot, the Fenians   *don't repeat it*
Papists
lazy lug-a-bouts,

Look, you're the Canadian. You don't understand
this place. You never lived here. Your mother – bless
her heart – never hurt anyone, always did right.

not that I'm against them all.
Take Mrs. Finnigan next door, she's
different, the way she helped our
wee Annie with the croup, wheezing
like it was her last, burning
up like a furnace.

But I wouldn't mix.

don't say it   don't
don't let it sit in my head muddle
my mind   don't
know it   didn't hear it
didn't   don't

64

Sure they're run by the priest
and who's going to feed all those children?

And us Protestants:
We don't kill people.

didn't   don't

Foreigners don't know a thing
about the troubles. No use talking. You've
no business writing. You've had too much book learning, mixing with
God knows who.

Do something useful with your education.

don't

WHAT IF A VOICE

I
What if a voice feels small,
doesn't want to say, doesn't
know how to sing, a voice in love
with song but without a tune, a throat clogged
up bad, words clunky and leaden, smell of
untold stories, unformed words stuck
mid-throat. No place to go.

What if a voice whines and attacks, picks
and prods, can find no good, can't keep
secrets, can't tell lies, can't hear
herself.

What if a voice wants to hide in a child's
choir gown, up in the balcony
at the candle-light service, middle
of the middle row so the words don't
matter, mouthing *Gloria* in the dark,
the tune her own.

What if the service is over but a voice
won't come down, wants only the balcony
and blown-out candles, hides under the pew
singing to herself, sleeps on a choir
gown pillow until light comes in through
the stained glass, humming the hymns by
heart.

II
What if a voice takes her own time, then
startles with rush and flow.

What if a voice wants new
snow, welcomes cool points on her tongue
falling, long and lapping, fresh
water in air, washing her face, single
flakes and clusters rushing earthbound, thick
along thin branches, cool song
melting, claiming and changing
the landscape.

CALLINGS

GONE TO SEED

Photo-figures burst out of frames and albums, dash
through the house, smash windows and doors, spar in
the kitchen, collide in the garden, shear the roses.
Cheese smiles and stern expressions fixed. Silent so

long, now they let loose: *How much did you make at
that job Father got you? Why did you get the house?
You drove the business into the ground. Get your smirk
and outdated clothes out of my face.* Husbands and

wives who knew each other too well, cousins who'd never
met but held grudges, sharpen garden tools. They spit
on their older, younger selves. Tipping compost beside
the pussy willows, they toss around moldy grapefruit

peels and rotten zucchinis. The aunts in Sunday best and
cousins in swimsuits attack the raspberries, wanting to be
the first to uproot them. Babies and old men, strong as
20-year-olds, swing hoes and spades at each other. They

rip the yellow fuzz off the pussy willows gone to
seed and rub it on each other, shrieking *Haa, Gotcha*,
as they streak and stain the remains of each other's
matte and glossy surfaces.

ALL I HAVE ARE PHOTOGRAPHS

Aunt Lucy's wedding, the guests in an arc
    across the road. I search for you among
       the stylish hats, the fox heads draped

around shoulders, the giggles – Uncle George
    has told another joke. Your script on the
       back of a tiny snapshot – *The Big Snowstorm*

1937. You're with your sister Evelyn and
    Uncle Mercer from New Zealand. He
       came back after forty years and his

bicycle was just where he'd left it, against
    the far wall of the barn. Your first time
       to see snow falling. Here you are –

First Winter in Canada 1948. Post war.
    Making a snowman with your sons who became
       Canadian sure as snow falls. Boys throwing

their first snowballs, white against the brick
    manse, lobbing them into maples. Snow fills
       the air, you can't taste enough of it.

A BIT OF A THRILL

One of those narrow meandering Irish roads
hedges on each side so high you can't see
if cars are coming, have to honk
when going around a curve, so hilly
and winding, there's a round curved mirror
to let you see what's coming
a bit of a thrill
especially if it's Uncle John Law
driving his son's six-cylinder
instead of his own Morris Minor
round a bend, over a hill, I'm bounced off Dad's lap
face up close to the windscreen.
Mum says, *Now, John, do you have to do a yearly driving test
once you reach eighty, the way they do in Canada?*

Ach no, not here, not till you have an accident.

THE NEW CROP

A new crop of young men
stands silent in the hall
tall like corn, their long
arms resting on the banister.
They are what's changed about the place.
Shrunken aunts say, *you're the image
of your mother.* My mother calls my daughter
by my name.

A row of my mother's sisters, her look-alikes,
gather at the mantle. Mother is
the tallest, they say, because she lay
in bed for a year with rheumatic fever.

My mother's mother used to shout
the men are in the yard! and
everyone would dash to get dinner on the table.
The only time my father heard her say an angry word:
my grandfather knocked over the churn
in the back kitchen. She used to make butter
because some men took creamery butter,
others took only home-made.

My uncle shows us around his house, points
out photographs, examines one –
a wedding scene. Exclaims
ach, it's me own.

SPEAK UP

Mum brings us a plate of shortbread bears, bunnies, baby chicks. Warm and ready, crisp at the edges, soft inside, looking at us with half-raisin eyes. We bite off heads and legs. A circle of girls in best party dresses, mine blue velvet: Mum helped me choose. We eat them slow, their little animal bodies first. Save the heads till last.

Now, I play my brother's tape, transferred from his old reel-to-reel. Press Start.

Father: Hello everyone, here we are in 1967, on an important day for a lovely young girl. We want you to be able to listen to this tape many years into the future. Who knows who will be listening to it?

Go on. Speak up. Tell us about your seventh birthday. Did you like your birthday? Who was at your party? What wonderful gifts did you get? What games did you play? Come on, speak up. What did you eat?

This was a very important year for you. You learned to read. Good for you. Now, let's have you read from your brand-new book, *A Child's Bible*. Here we have something very important: The Ten Commandments. Go ahead. Read.

Daughter: Honour your Mother and Father.

Father: Now, wait, you know Father comes first. Father and Mother. Father.

From the kitchen doorway Mum's voice sings small. *Happy Birthday, Sweetie.* Her netted party apron tied at the back. A double strand of crystal beads against her deep green dress.

Her tune reaches for me now as I approach the age she was. Her tone. Her voice clear through static. A stray note.

HER CALLING

Where is her voice? Hiding in hatboxes,
between feathers, between the velvet bow
and the elastic. Where is she with her singsong
lilt? In the glue where she stuck the handle
back on her Belleek china teacup. In
the hushed fibres of this sweater she

washed and wore and washed again. In between the lines
of her letters, in the straight up-and-down of her tidy script,
the tiny extravagance of a flourished ending, the crinkle
of the silver wrapping she took off the Kit Kat, two fingers
for me, two for her, in the rev of the plane's
engine, down the runway, next stop Belfast, home

coming, in the phone ringing, which in my dream is her
calling to hear about her granddaughter's choir
performance, or announcing her return, by plane,
next Tuesday, Aer Lingus, she'd walk in the door,
take a feather duster and a brass gong from
her suitcase, in her shushing the baby, rushing

the baby along the hall to the bedroom, so her
cries won't be heard, in the big loud voice she'd
use to stop the train if I was left
on the platform, she'd stop it cold. Then she'd know
what she was meant to do, a calling of
her own. She'd always loved men

in uniforms, but better yet herself, peaked hat, she'd be
the conductor, away she'd go, she'd a job to do, her voice
ringing *Belleville, Kingston, Brockville, Cornwall,* she
would summon whole cities, the train whistle
blowing. To see if they were listening, she'd drop in
Dusty Doorknob, just after *Smith Falls,* sing out *Morning*

Glory, Nice'n'Easy, Johnnie-Jump-Up, Shake'n'Bake. She'd
call them out on the way to Montreal and the passengers
couldn't wait for them on the way back to Toronto, they'd
shout them out too: *one, two, three, Long Necked Goose.*
She'd tip her hat and stop that train. New towns would spring up
at her suggestion: *Peace,* a tiny village but worth a stop,

Tranquility, with a station at its outskirts. *Lusty Lovers* —
eager couples would leap from the train.
Eternity. Fecundity. She'd see them coming, would love
the sound of their names. The train whistle blowing, her
engine gaining.

Who needs all this Mum stuff? A little black notebook, recipe for beauty lotion, notes on whether Women's Institute members in Hillsborough, in 1953, had paid their two and six pence. (Mrs. Henry hadn't.)

Trouble is I can't part with it: her letters to me, from me, the cards I made her, *Get Better Soon* and the school-made *To A Wonderful Mum*. Could I call them period pieces? The telegram she received when her mother died, speeches she made at United Church Women's meetings? Memorabilia overload, detritus maximus. Hatboxes, shoeboxes, shopping bags full.

What can I do? Squirrel it away under the bed? Could I send envelopes of her hair to my brothers, one of her old address books to each? I could parcel them up in her best aprons, but will I know they've arrived safely?

I've started my own museum. It was all I could do. Right out there in the garage. At first a few kind friends came, then the neighbours. Start small and manageable, they say. Let your obsessions work for you. I took the course for new women entrepreneurs, I'm going to get a loan. I'm making the right home for Mum's teacups, bed jackets, bobby pins, napkin ring.

How will I pitch it? *My Mother, A Contemporary of the Queen.* Or shorter, *The Queen and My Ma*, that bit of an Irish ring, very popular these days. When it catches on, I'll buy back her last home: give suburbia a museum of its own.

Visitors can trace their own roots. Heritage charts made while you wait. Saturday mornings will be Irish dance for kids. The first museum with properly made tea: start by heating the teapot. Soda farl, wheaten bannock made on the premises. In time, I'll get a licence for Guinness on tap. You'll never catch me selling plastic leprechauns, or *Kiss Me, I'm Irish* buttons. Penny whistles? Bottled Holy Water? Bricks of peat from the homeland?

Look, we're talking real history here, primary sources: Mum's recipes, postcards, 1950's prayers for the missionaries in India. A glass case labeled: *All Spectacles Worn Since Arrival in Canada.* Laminated doctor's records. I'll practise my calligraphy, make labels galore. Our family photos can't end up in a pawnshop.

Dad and the brothers might not approve, but it could even give Dad a place to preach, Sundays at 11 AM if he wants. Dad and the boys will be proud when I make this profitable.

School trips will come, I'll supply the clipboards with worksheets, projects on immigration, the role of women in the church, the Troubles. Mum's Museum (Mum's for short) will thrive, get written up. Archivists will flock to help. I'll read up on preservation, conservation, whichever – no bugs or rot will destroy our artefacts. My mum is a kind of Everymum.

A museum to change lives. I'll write a book on how to start your own Mum's Museum. The idea will grow and we wouldn't have to wait till our mums are dead. Living Mums can join right in. They can sit down in their own display cases, telling it like it is.

SHE STARTED TO SHED

after her mother stopped breathing, after her mother's body, which she loved more than her own, was no longer in the world and she was no longer washing her mother's back, easing her out of the bath-tub, checking if she had taken her pills, making secret calls to the home care, plotting how to fatten her bones. eat please

she started to shed skin when she gave birth to a daughter, a breech baby. she and the baby had kept a secret from everyone, not letting on that the baby would come bum first until mother and baby pushed their way into the world, upsetting the apple cart and the doctors. afterwards both were that bit braver and bolder

Canada Day: she was sitting on a bank in the park listening to the Celtic fiddle. she wasn't young or old after all, there was nothing she had to do, she was shedding fast, old skin cracking, flaking, falling from her in strips, until she noticed the sure shape of her hip, the life returning to her breasts now that she was done with nursing

she peeled off her favourite sweater, once her mother's, sun on her new skin smooth

I'VE GOT MY MOTHER'S 1950S SMILE

plastered to my face and it isn't
doing a damn bit of good. Hey,
Mum, it isn't keeping your family
together. And it isn't smiling down on

Hillsborough, the Garvaghy Road, Belfast,
three child-sized coffins edging up a hill.
Nor on this heated-up city, pregnant student
on welfare dying under house arrest. Nor on

the women's shelter making ends meet on the
money Bill Gates spent on yesterday's lunch. Nor
is it going to help the baby born in Tent City or
her parents when Children's Aid butts in, puts

the state's hands all over their creation. Just keep
smiling. *Have a good day!* It isn't helping children
with cancer in Baghdad or Basra. Nor the woman
sleeping from Lansdowne till the end of the line, her

home tumbling from a plastic bag. Look, Maria, *The Hills
are Alive* if you can get out of the city. On the wrong side
of the tracks – the women have lost their teeth. Sure as Miss
Goody Two Shoes I keep the neighbour from spitting at my

children – gotta make some use of a pretty face and white
middle-class teeth. Smiling and mentioning a respectable job keeps
the parent-teacher interview chipper. I can wheedle my children
a little protection. Their milk teeth, my eye-teeth. Can I build

a poem with teeth? All we chew, spit out. A smashed smile
dropping teeth. Teeth tinkling. Porcelain. Pavement.

The Line That Keeps You Safe

You don't see the line. Our plane disappearing, Granny's with you. You are busy doing the fuzzy felt farm puzzle. You've cut out stamp-size rectangles of paper to be letters in the farm mailbox. *That's mine*, you said, pointing out the letter from Santa – the one in cheery typing which makes no promises.

We are the line between here and gone, between speaking and not, the line between the moment you hit another car and the moment you swerve and miss it. Between loving you too much and loving you right as rain.

A 1964 line made by a knife cutting open my mother's chest, straight down between her breasts. Took out her heart. The line between the moment when her heart was kept beating and when it started to beat on its own. The straight line of the sheets turned down and tucked in as I lay in the single bed that night at the Chalmers' house on Eire Street. They kept a light on in the hall and the door open a crack.

Next day the bad nurse didn't let children into Intensive Care. But the day after, the good nurse did. The Queen of Hearts and the Queen of Clubs.

Us kids posing for a photograph, the boys in their black pants and white shirts, me in my plaid dress – grey in this black and white snap. My brother's arm around my shoulder.

We are the white line disappearing across the sky, the skipping rope stretched so tight it snaps and someone falls over. The line between going away and coming back.

VISITATION V

She came bearing paradise cakes, angel-food
cake with raspberry sauce, sponge cake with orange

filling, lemon loaf. We hadn't had dessert
in months, she knew we were starving. Spicy

pumpkin loaf, carrot cake, and egg custard she
made on arrival, all the ingredients tucked

into her skirt. We must have known she was coming:
we'd prepared the banquet hall, candles lit

at each round table, night and snow falling. Eating
on and on, we served each other delicacies on blue

plates, palm leaves, white doilies, a dusting of
icing sugar, scribble of chocolate sauce. All the family

getting along famously, no need to remember who was who.
We fed her too. We shifted to a new table for each new

sampling, dishes piling around us, we scorned cutlery,
flinging it over our shoulders. Our fingers fell on

hazelnut torte. We grew round and content, so sleepy.
At last, we sat in splendidly stuffed armchairs and

couldn't reach the table. We took turns rising and feeding
each other morsels, choosing from triangles of baklava,

ladhus, sips of coconut milk. We settled back lazily, passing
each other glass bowls of kiwis, sections of tangerine, plump

cranberries, pomegranate seeds, dates dripping honey, slices of
heaven, slivers of earth, promises.

BETWEEN SOCKS AND SHIRTS

How's the sky for laundry? The air for messages? No more email/fax/
voice-mail/cell-phone. I'll wheel out a message to you with my laundry,

between socks and shirts, summer sun tickling the hairs on my arms.
I like an excuse to get outside, raise my arms with damp sheets, meditate

on all the sun can do while I'm not looking. Go to your clothesline, late
afternoon, your clothes warmed and aired. Reel in the line, savour

its squeak and groan. Unpeg my voice, let it unfurl among your darks or
lights, place the laundry basket on the couch beside you. Wheel in

a sun-licked line.

WALK ON OVER TO HIGH PARK

                               or hop the streetcar west.
Find a river bank if you're lucky. Climb to the bench

on the hilltop, Lake Ontario, Grenadier Pond shine in
your gaze. Rest against the plaque: *In Memoriam,*

At Peace with Nature at Last. Rub against bronze and wood.
Then, be done with words, not a word out of you, not a word

in front of you: not a sailboat, fleck of white on blue, not a man
casting his fishing line again, not a syringe by the curb, not

those tall apartments, an endless stream of traffic, not a word
you should have said, could have said, meant to say.

                               Black oak and cherry,
Great Blue Heron.

GLOSSARY

craic – chat or conversation

schoch – gutter or trench by the side of the road

soda farl – white flour buttermilk bread in a round flat-cake shape

wheaten – whole wheat buttermilk bread

whin – broom, a kind of bush

ACKNOWLEDGEMENTS

My thanks to everyone at Sage Hill Writing Experience and the Banff Centre for the Arts, the instructors, co-ordinators, staff and fellow participants. At Sage Hill, the hat began to stop the train, thanks to the careful signalling of Don McKay, and Jeanette Lynes, Miranda Pearson, Sandy Shreve, and Adam Sol. At Banff, I learned more from Don's insight and from the careful ear of Daphne Marlatt.

A huge wave of my hat to Honor Ford-Smith, Christine Higdon, Maureen Hynes, Allison MacDuffee, Ruth Roach Pierson, John Oughton, Noreen Shanahan, Betsy Trumpener, and Liz Ukrainetz for reading various versions of this manuscript and helping me find what was trying to emerge. Thank you to the writers who have brought their fine poetic sense to so many of these poems: Martha Baillie, Julie Berry, Rosemary Blake, Mary Lou Soutar-Hynes, Susana Molinolo, Patria Rivera, Megan Williams, and Elana Wolff. For nudging me towards this book, thank you to Kelley Aitken, Christine Almeida, and Rena Ginsberg.

Hats off to my first writing teachers, Rhea Tregebov and Helen Humphreys. And to Di Brandt and Michael Redhill for their encouragement.

Thank you to my father, William Stewart, for his love of words.

My deepest thanks to my partner, Richard Pathak.

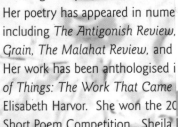

Sheila Stewart grew up in Stratford, Wate
Her poetry has appeared in nume
including *The Antigonish Review,*
Grain, The Malahat Review, and
Her work has been anthologised i
of Things: The Work That Came
Elisabeth Harvor. She won the 2(
Short Poem Competition. Sheila lives in Toronto and
works on adult literacy issues at the Ontario Institute for
Studies in Education of the University of Toronto.

Tight and tighter, the mother binding her daughter to her, the
daughter binding the mother's aching legs. Sheila Stewart "puts
down words to get closer" to a mother whose ashes are away in
Ireland, but she achieves much more than a remembrance – this
is a collection of tight, spare poems laced with Celtic wit,
wry and askance, and astonishing imagery for the
complexities of family. Stewart has a confident
command of poetic form, and these poems
are honed sharp enough to prickle
your eyes, startle your heart.
– *Maureen Hynes*

Stewart's living "Mum's Museum" offers
a gentle interrogation of family stories, probing
between the sayable for what couldn't be said, for threads of
dis/connection, glimpses of remembered feasts, "dates dripping
honey, slices of heaven, slivers of earth, promises." A shy love
song; a tender poetic debut.   – *Di Brandt*

Sheila Stewart traces and retraces the complex geography of grief
until its contours come clear in these angry, loving poems of loss
and reclamation.
                                                – *Rhea Tregebov*

ISBN 0-919897-89-4
Wolsak and Wynn

9 780919 897892